For the children of Dunblane School

Text copyright © 1997 by Ann Pilling
Illustrations copyright © 1997 by Michael Foreman

First U.S. edition 1997

Library of Congress Cataloging-in-Publication Data
Pilling, Ann.
Creation : read-aloud stories from many lands / retold by Ann Pilling ;
illustrated by Michael Foreman.
Includes bibliographical references.
ISBN 1-56402-888-7
1. Creation—Comparative studies—Juvenile literature.
2. Creation—Mythology—Juvenile literature. I. Foreman, Michael, date, ill. II. Title.
BL325.C7P55   1997
291.2'4—dc20   96-38745

2 4 6 8 10 9 7 5 3 1

Printed in Italy

This book was typeset in Goudy.
The pictures were done in watercolor and ink.

Candlewick Press
2067 Massachusetts Avenue
Cambridge, Massachusetts 02140

CREATION

Read-Aloud Stories from Many Lands

CREATION

Read-Aloud Stories from Many Lands

retold by
ANN PILLING

illustrated by
MICHAEL FOREMAN

CANDLEWICK PRESS
CAMBRIDGE, MASSACHUSETTS

CONTENTS

INTRODUCTION
»→•←«
6

THE CREATION OF THE WORLD
»→•←«
9

HOW THE WORLD CAME FROM AN EGG
A Story from China
10

HOW THE WORLD WAS MADE IN SEVEN DAYS
A Story from the Bible
13

HOW A TURTLE CARRIED THE WORLD
From the Seneca Tribe of North America
17

HOW EVERYTHING CAME FROM FIRE AND ICE
A Norse Myth
22

HOW A LONELY GODDESS FILLED THE WORLD WITH PEOPLE
A Story from China
27

WARMTH AND LIGHT

—✦➤•◄✦—

31

HOW THE WORLD WAS LIT UP
BY A BONFIRE
An Australian Aboriginal Story

32

HOW THE SUN BECAME
BRIGHTER THAN THE MOON
A Story from the Cameroons

38

HOW A GIRL BROUGHT ABOUT
THE SEASONS
A Greek Myth

42

HOW SUMMER WAS BROUGHT
INTO WINTER'S HOME
From the Algonquian Tribe of North America

50

HOW A CROW BROUGHT
DAYLIGHT INTO A DARK LAND
A Story from the Inuit People

55

HOW A BROOMSTICK
BRIGHTENED THE WORLD
A Story from Sri Lanka

62

CREATURES GREAT AND SMALL

—✦➤•◄✦—

65

WHY RABBIT IS SHY
From the Hopi Tribe of North America

67

WHY SNAKE HAS NO LEGS
An Ashanti Story from Ghana

73

WHY THE BEAR HAS A STUMPY TAIL
A Story from Norway

80

WHY ELEPHANTS LIVE
IN THE JUNGLE
From the Kamba People of Kenya

84

WHY THERE ARE BUTTERFLIES
An Australian Aboriginal Story

88

BIBLIOGRAPHY

——✦➤•◄✦——

96

INTRODUCTION

Since human beings first appeared on the earth they have been asking questions about it. Who or What made the world? Where did the people come from? And the sun? And the moon and stars? Why do we have summer and winter? There are many thousands of stories from all over the world that have tried to give the answers. Perhaps a giant came out of an egg and created the universe. Or was it a woman who fell through a rip in the sky? Did it all start as a battle between some giants, or did God simply say, "Let there be light!"?

The stories in this book not only address huge questions about the universe, they focus on small things, too. In nearly all creation stories birds, animals, and fish appear on earth before human beings, and they play important parts, sometimes showing more wisdom than mankind. But not always. Why, for example, does the bear, one of our biggest mammals, have such a silly little tail? Why are rabbits always so nervous and shy? There are deeper questions, too. How did sorrow first come into the world? Why does everything have to die?

Some of the stories, like those from ancient Greece and from the Norse peoples, are very sophisticated and poetic, inhabited by magnificent, brooding gods. Others are much more everyday. One tells how an impatient servant girl sweeps the sky out of her way while she is brushing the floor. How different this is from the magisterial account in the Bible where God separates light from dark. Different again is the Inuit account of the clever crow who steals light from a baby in an igloo and flies away with it on a string.

The stories here are not always very logical and are sometimes charmingly contradictory. For example, in the Senecan account of the creation of the world, a woman falls through a hole in the sky and plunges into the dark emptiness called Chaos, a world where humans have yet to be created. But, unlike the Chinese or biblical accounts, we already have a fully formed person! So, who made *her*? Nobody has attempted to tidy up these accounts or to make everything fit neatly together, and this strengthens the feeling that they are genuine. The untidiness exists because they are so very ancient and because the stories were told by word of mouth, around the campfire, or at Grandmother's knee. They were not written down on paper but passed from one generation to another, so the details often got mixed up.

This book does not pretend to be a complete collection of stories about how things came to be. That would fill many volumes and take a lifetime to put together. This is simply a group of stories about creation that I hope you will enjoy because they are *good* stories. Some are grand and some are terrifying. Many are beautiful. Others are a bit cheeky and will make you laugh. All, I hope, will teach you something because, like a good poem, a really good story "begins in delight and ends in wisdom."

Ann Pilling

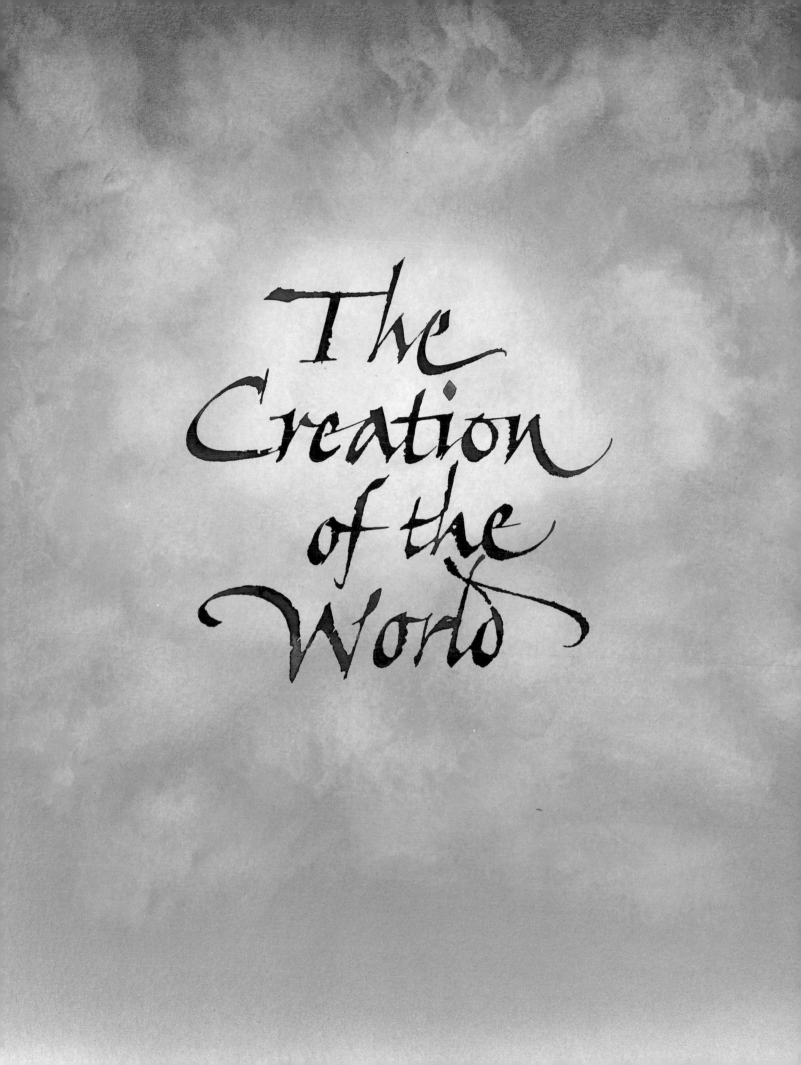

HOW THE WORLD CAME FROM AN EGG

A STORY FROM CHINA

ONCE THERE WAS NOTHING at all but a very large egg. Where had it come from? There was certainly no hen to lay it.

For thousands of years the egg just *was*. Then . . . *scratch scratch. Clickety-click . . . POP!* It broke into two pieces and out stepped a giant.

One half of the egg dropped downward and became *yin*, which means "earth." The other half floated upward and became *yang*, which means "sky." The giant, whose name was Phan-Ku, trod the earth down very firmly and pushed at the sky with his hands. This way he kept them separate. Then he started to grow, and as he grew, the gap between earth and sky became bigger and bigger.

Every day Phan-Ku grew ten feet taller and this growing went on for eighteen thousand years. But in the end he

became very tired, holding up the whole sky, and anyway, there was more to do before he died.

Carefully he felt the earth, then the sky. Both seemed firmly in place. So he dropped his arms and took a rest. Then he set about shaping the world, hollowing out valleys with his enormous hands and tracing the paths of winding rivers with his huge fingers.

It was such hard work and he was now so very old that Phan-Ku started to cry. His tears rolled down, filling the rivers and streams to overflowing.

At last he lay down. He was so tired that he wanted to sleep forever. As he died, his left eye became the sun and his right eye the moon; his bones turned into rocks and precious stones, and his hair became trees and plants and shrubs. Not a speck of his enormous body was wasted.

Phan-Ku was not forgotten after his death. When man eventually appeared on earth and heard thunder and lightning, they knew it was the sound of the giant's voice. But he never came back to the world he had created. He had died to give it life. And the people were lonely without their creator. That is how sadness first came into the world.

->>●<-<-

How the World Was Made in Seven Days

IN THE BEGINNING, God made the heaven and the earth. But at first the earth was shapeless and empty, and everything was covered with thick darkness.

So God said, "Let there be light!" And there was light.

God saw that it was good, so he separated it from the darkness. He called the light "day" and the darkness "night."

Then God made the sky over the great waters that covered the earth, gathering them together in one place so that dry land appeared. And on this land he set plants and trees growing, and it all seemed very good.

Then lights were put in the sky like great lamps—the sun, the moon, and the stars—to give us the seasons and to make night and day. Into the sea God put all kinds of fish, and birds to fly above them in the air.

"Have young," he said to them all, "and fill this earth of mine to overflowing."

Then he said, "Let the dry land be filled with animals, both large and small, those that walk and creep and jump and run." And it all seemed very good indeed.

At last, God made man himself, and man was special, because he looked more like God than any other creature God had made. He was so special that he was put in charge

of all the things that now filled the marvelous new world—the plants and the herbs, the trees and their fruits, the fish and the birds, and all the creeping, running, jumping things. And God blessed him.

"Rule the earth and its creatures that I have made," he said. "They are for you."

Then God looked all around and felt that creation was very good indeed. It had taken six long days to make it, so on the seventh day he rested.

And that is why the seventh day of the week is a holy day, because it is when God rested from all his work.

✦➤•◄✦

How a Turtle Carried the World

In the beginning, there was no earth to live on, but up above, in the Great Blue, there was a woman who dreamed dreams. One night she dreamed about a tree covered with white blossoms, a tree that brightened up the sky when its flowers opened but that brought terrible darkness when they closed again. The dream frightened her, so she went and told it to the wise old men who lived with her, in their village in the sky.

"Pull up this tree," she begged them, but they did not understand. All they did was to dig around its roots, to make space for more light. But the tree just fell through the hole they had made and disappeared. After that there was no light at all, only darkness.

The old men grew frightened of the woman and her dreams. It was her fault that the light had gone away forever.

So they dragged her toward the hole and pushed her through as well. Down, down she fell, down toward a great emptiness. There was nothing below her but a heaving waste of water and she would surely have been smashed to pieces, this strange dreaming woman from the Great Blue, had not a fish hawk come to her aid. His feathers made a pillow for her and she drifted gently above the waves.

But the fish hawk could not keep her up all on his own. He needed help. So he called out to the creatures of the deep. "We must find some firm ground for this poor

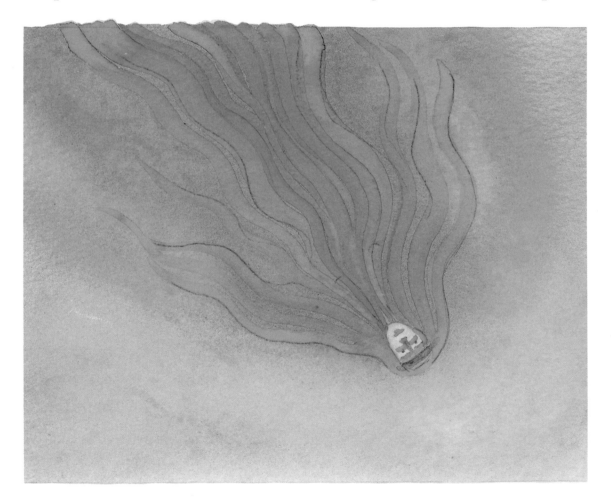

woman to rest on," he said anxiously. But there was no ground, only the swirling, endless waters.

A helldiver went down, down, down to the very bottom of the sea and brought back a little bit of mud in his beak. He found a turtle, smeared the mud onto its back, and dived down again for more.

Then the ducks joined in. They loved getting muddy and they too brought beakfuls of the ocean floor and spread it over the turtle's shell. The beavers helped—they were great builders—and they worked away, making the shell bigger and bigger.

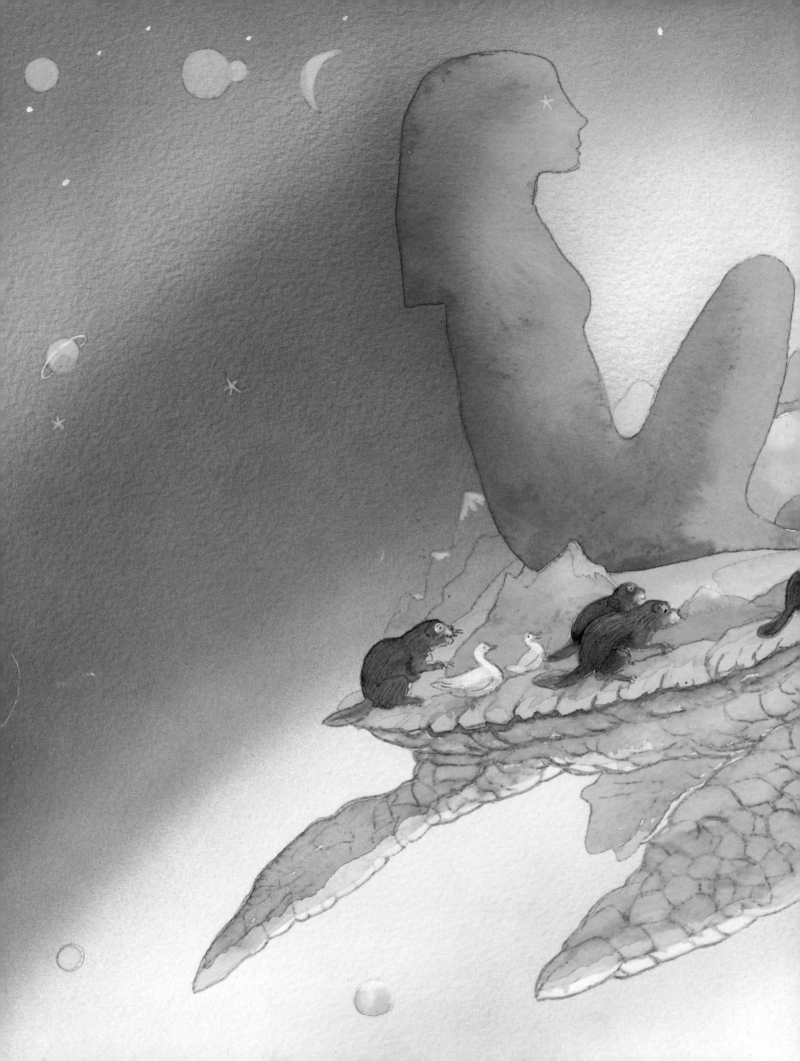

Everybody was very busy now and everybody was excited. This world they were making seemed to be growing *enormous*! The birds and the animals rushed about building countries, then continents, until, in the end, they had made the whole round earth, while all the time the sky woman was safely sitting on the turtle's back.

And the turtle holds the earth up to this very day.

How Everything Came from Fire and Ice

A Norse Myth

At first there was nothing at all—no earth, no sea, no sky, no grass. Then a land of freezing shadows began to form in the far, far north. It was called Niflheim and out of it spurted a great fountain from which flowed twelve rivers. The name of this fountain was Hvergelmir and its waters were icy cold.

In the south another land was taking shape. This was called Muspell. It was fiery hot and it had rivers whose waters were full of poison that frothed on the top like yeast. Where these waters entered the cold land of Niflheim they thickened and slowed down. Soon they had turned into solid ice. And that was all there was at first, just fire and ice. Nothing could grow, not even a blade of grass. There was little hope for a human race.

But then, after long ages, warm air from Muspell blew

across the empty world and began to melt the towering ice blocks of Niflheim.

Out of the biggest block came a giant, not quickly—he had been locked in the ice for millions of years—but stretching and yawning and looking around to make mischief. This was Ymir the Roarer, the first of all living things.

He was hungry and thirsty, so he roared. Out of the ice came a cow called Audumla, the very first animal.

Ymir drank her warm milk while she licked at the ice. (She liked it because it tasted so salty.) As she licked, her warm breath started to melt it and Ymir saw that a shape was emerging—first some hair, then a head, and, very slowly, the body of another being like himself. This was Buri, whose son, Bor, was the father of Odin, the mightiest god of all.

Meanwhile, Audumla went on peacefully licking at the ice, releasing the sleeping gods from their glittering prisons. When they were all free they stood apart, great towering shapes of silence, waiting to see what would happen next in the making of this new world.

Odin knew that Ymir was too dangerous to stay alive, so with the help of his brothers, he hacked the giant to death. The blood that spurted out of him was creamy white, because of all the milk he had drunk. This flowed across the great emptiness that lay between the lands of fire and ice and turned into the sea.

Out of Ymir's dead body they made earth, calling it Midgard—"the yard in the middle." His flesh became land, his bones became mountains, and his hair turned into trees. They took his skull and raised it on four enormous pillars, and this became the sky. To make sun, moon, and stars they gathered together sparks that had flown out of Muspell and set them in the heavens. Soon the sun began to warm Midgard and grass started to grow.

But the new world still lacked people. One day, while traveling with his brothers, Odin found two fallen trees. Slowly he raised them up, breathing life into them, while his brothers clothed them with flesh, then giving them the gifts of reason and understanding.

From these two new beings, whom they named Embla and Ask, sprang the entire human race.

But the story is not without sadness. Three woman giants, hearing that Odin had created some people, came together at the foot of Yggdrasil, the everlasting tree that holds up the dome of the sky. They were jealous creatures and they wanted to make sure that these new beings did not live forever, as they did.

So they picked up some pieces of wood that had fallen from Yggdrasil and began to cut at them, making notches that signified for each human being the day of its birth. Then they carved strange patterns describing exactly what would happen in its life.

There were many, many patterns because all kinds of wonderful and strange things were to happen to mankind. But they never forgot to make the last notch. This was the deepest of all and it meant death. Without it the new beings might challenge the gods, becoming too powerful and too wise. And that is how sorrow came into the world.

-+->-•-<-+-

How a Lonely Goddess Filled the World with People

------ ⇥•⇤ ------

A Story from China

THE WORLD WAS MADE by Phan-Ku the giant but he did not make any people. There were gods and goddesses and some very strange monsters but nobody human at all. It was a beautiful place but it was a lonely one.

The goddess Nuwa wanted people around her. Although she had a dragon's tail, her upper body was that of a human being, and she wanted to talk to humans and to share their thoughts. Most of all she wanted to love them. So she went and sat on the banks of the great Yellow River.

The bed of the river was very muddy. After a while she bent down and scooped up some of the mud in her hand. Then she began to make something. She shaped a body and she shaped a head. She shaped arms and hands and

fingers and stuck them all together. She was just about to make a dragon's tail like her own when she grew thoughtful. Legs would be much more useful, she decided. So she made some and stuck them on.

All this took a long time because Nuwa had worked very carefully. When the little mud figure was finished, she sat it down on the riverbank, breathed life into it, and gave it a gentle push.

At first it tottered and swayed about, then it started to walk, trying out its brand-new legs. Soon it was running and leaping and dancing around. "Mother!" it shouted gleefully. "Look at me!"

Nuwa was delighted and at once set about making some more mud dolls. But it took a very long time and the world was a big place to fill with people. She decided she would have to take a shortcut to speed everything up. After all, she *was* a goddess.

She found a stick and stuck it into the mud. Then she pulled it out again and shook it very hard so that all the mud came off in little drops. As the sun dried them, each one became a little person and ran around. Some say that the most intelligent people were shaped by Nuwa's own hands, but that everybody else was created out of the mud drops scattered by the stick.

Some of the people were men and some of them were women. She told them to live together and have families to fill the world. After all, she could not go on making mud dolls forever.

-+->-●-<+-

Warmth
and
Light

decided they should have it every single day. So he gathered together all the other spirits and they set about collecting sticks, which they heaped up into an enormous bonfire. The plan was to light a fire in the sky every morning so that the creatures on earth could see properly.

Knowing that the animals might be frightened by this sudden strange light, the good spirit first lit the morning star. He thought that when they saw it they would know that the sun was about to shine.

But when the star appeared, the animals were still fast asleep. So the spirit went to the kookaburra bird, whose loud harsh cry could be heard above the voice of any other creature.

"Do something for me," he said. "When you see the morning star, cry out with all your strength. Your voice will wake up all the animals, and they won't be frightened when the new sun starts to blaze in the sky."

So the kookaburra opened his enormous beak very wide.

"Gou-gour-gah-gah!" he shrieked. "Gou-gour-gah-gah!"

All the animals stirred in their sleep, blinked around, stretched themselves, and looked up into the sky. There was the gentle morning star, and as they watched, the sky slowly turned from black to gray, then to pink, then to red and gold, brighter and brighter as the flames of the huge bonfire licked at the dry wood, leaping up into a vast blaze that lit the whole earth.

The fire grew bigger and hotter by the minute. The animals enjoyed this new "sun"—the warmth of it and the light. They noticed that at noon the sky bonfire was at its biggest and hottest, and that, as the spirits let the flames die out, the earth became cooler and the light in the sky began to grow dim. In the evening, all that remained was a dull red glow, which was sunset. Then the good spirit took some clouds and carefully wrapped them around the dying embers, putting them away in a safe place until the next morning, when he used them to start the fire again.

The kookaburra went on crying and screeching before sunrise, telling the world that the sun was about to come up, and when there were people on earth, mothers told their children not to laugh at him. He was so funny with his great big beak and his horrible voice. But they gave a warning. "If you say nasty things about Kookaburra," they said, "you will hurt his feelings. Then he might go away and sulk, and if he did, the sun wouldn't come up anymore, ever again."

Think of that!

→>●<←

How the Sun Became Brighter Than the Moon

A Story from the Cameroons

When the world was still very new, the sun and the moon were equals and shone with the same brightness. They were good friends and often went around together. But one day everything changed.

They had decided to take their families bathing in the river. The sun took his family out of sight around a bend so they could get ready for their swim in private. (In those days everybody was very polite.)

"I'll jump in first," said the sun to the moon, as he went off. "You'll know I'm in the water when it starts to boil."

But as soon as the sun was out of sight, he ordered his children to cut down branches from the trees. "Set fire to them," he said, "and throw them into the river." So they did.

38

The minute the moon saw the water bubbling and boiling, he jumped in. As he swam about, clouds of steam swirled around his head. It was very hot indeed.

When he climbed out again, the moon discovered he had turned very pale. He was frosty and cold and his brilliance was only a shadow of what it had been before.

The sun mocked him. "Now I will always be brighter than you," he jeered. "We didn't go swimming at all!" It was a very cruel trick and the moon decided there and then that he would have his revenge.

Time passed and a great famine came upon the earth. Every day people were dying. The moon saw his chance to get even with the sun. But he hid his anger and paid the sun a visit.

"We must kill our children," he said, "if we are to survive. There are too many people to feed. Some must be sacrificed. I shall take my family upstream, where you once bathed in the river, and I shall kill them all. When you see the water running with blood you will know that they are dead. Then you must start killing yours."

The sun agreed and when he saw that the river had turned red, he killed every member of his family and threw their bodies into the water. But the moon had done something very cruel. He had not killed his family at all. He had merely told his children to throw handfuls of red clay into the river, to make it look like blood.

The sun, who had once had so many wives and children, was now alone. And he is still alone, shining up there in the sky in great majesty. The moon is much less bright but he still has all of his family. These are the crowds of stars that shine with him, night after night.

How a Girl Brought About the Seasons

A Greek Myth

When the world was new it had no seasons. There was no winter and no summer. Then a girl named Persephone was carried off to hell by a lonely god, and everything changed. This is what happened.

In the beginning, three gods ruled over creation. King Zeus ruled the sky and his brother Poseidon the sea. The land under the earth was ruled by Hades. He was the loneliest of the gods. Only dead people ever came to visit him. He wanted a wife and he chose the beautiful Persephone.

She was the daughter of a powerful goddess named Demeter, who gave life to everything that grew in the world. All the gods feared her, and Zeus knew she would never let her daughter marry Hades; but the dark sad god who lived under the earth had fallen in love with

Persephone and he was determined to make her his wife.

One day she went picking flowers on the slopes of Mount Etna. Zeus had made a secret plan to help Hades capture his bride, and he caused a miraculous white narcissus flower to burst into blossom at her feet. A hundred blooms grew from its single stem and its sweet scent seemed to fill the whole of creation. With a cry of delight, Persephone bent down to pick it.

As she touched its petals there was a hideous noise behind her. The earth shook and the ground beneath her feet split open. Up from his dark kingdom rode Hades, the god of hell, driving a great black chariot pulled by four plunging black horses. Roaring with triumph, he swept up the terrified young girl and vanished into the gaping hole in the mountainside. The rocky jaws closed up and nothing was left but the white narcissus flower.

Demeter knew that her daughter had been carried away. She had heard the girl's cry of terror, echoing around the mountains, and she set off at once to look for her, never stopping to rest, taking nothing at all to eat nor to drink.

Day and night she wandered, calling Persephone's name. Then she heard that Zeus, the king of the gods, had helped Hades with his cruel plan. She was very angry and went away to a lonely temple in a place called Eleusis, where she dressed in the rags of an old woman and spent her days weeping for her beloved daughter.

Nothing new grew on earth because Demeter, the mother of all that lives, had withdrawn her power. Crops were sown but came to nothing and cattle pulled their plows across the fields in vain. All over the world people began to starve. Zeus sent many messengers to the heart-broken goddess. "The people are dying," he said, "because nothing will grow. Take up your work again, I beg you." But Demeter would not listen.

Finally Zeus sent Hermes, his own special messenger, down to the underworld. Hermes knew the way because it was he who guided the dead on their last journey. He took off his winged sandals, cast aside the slender gold wand he used to mark the path, and stood in front of Hades' black marble throne. Little Persephone looked so pale and fragile compared with her dark and silent husband, like a tiny flower growing bravely in hell.

"Hades," he said, "have pity on us all. Demeter mourns for her daughter and nothing on earth will grow. There is no food left to eat and the people are starving. Let your wife return to her mother, I beg of you."

For a long time Hades did not speak. He loved Persephone and she had eased his loneliness. But he was a god and a god should have mercy on mortal man. He climbed down from his throne, put his wife's hand into the hand of Hermes, and turned away sadly.

How Summer Was Brought into Winter's Home

FROM THE ALGONQUIAN TRIBE OF NORTH AMERICA

GLOOSKAP, THE MIGHTY GOD, once went on a very long journey, northward, to the land of ice. When he was too tired to take another step, he stopped to ask for shelter at a great white wigwam. It was encrusted with jewels made of frozen snowflakes, all glittering across the dark. It was the home of Winter, the famous giant.

Winter made him very welcome, lighting a pipe for him and sitting him down while he told him old stories about the days gone by. Glooskap grew drowsy as he sat listening. The drone of the giant's voice was casting a spell on him, and he was getting colder and colder.

Soon he had drifted off into a sleep so deep that he only woke up when Giant Winter crept away and left him alone.

Then Glooskap set off for the south. As he walked along he felt the earth getting warmer. Flowers were springing up and a bird was singing somewhere.

In a forest he came across some little people dancing under the trees. The most beautiful of them all was a tiny girl named Summer; she was their queen. Glooskap bent down and took her in his hand. Then, from the skin of a moose, he made a long lasso, which he tied around her waist. He wanted to take the beautiful creature with him, and he was anxious that she might escape.

Her friends ran after him. "Bring back our queen!" they cried, and their little voices set the tall trees ringing.

But Glooskap hurried on his way, paying out his long lasso with Summer firmly tied to it. He was determined not to let his treasure go.

In time, he went back to visit Giant Winter and again the old man told him stories. But this time Glooskap had the greater power because Summer was with him, tucked safely inside his coat. She was small and delicate but in her own quiet way she was strong. As Winter listened to Glooskap's stories he began to feel very strange, faint and weak with great beads of sweat standing out on his forehead, his power ebbing away from him, his wigwam dissolving. He cried out in bewilderment but found that he had no voice anymore. The ice giant himself was melting away.

The world was warming up. The melting snow carried away the dead brown winter leaves and on the riverbanks new shoots were showing, all green and tender. The birds had started to build their nests.

Out from their hiding places crept the little people Glooskap had met in the forest. The spring had come and that meant their queen had returned to them. "Go," said Glooskap softly, and he turned his steps toward the south while the little people rejoiced together, like so many singing birds.

→►●◄←

How a Crow Brought Daylight into a Dark Land

A Story from the Inuit People

IN THE FAR, FAR NORTH, where the Inuit live, it is dark for six months of the year and for the other six months it is light. This is the story of how that came to be.

At the beginning, the Inuit did not know what daylight was because it was always dark. All they had to see by were little lamps of seal oil. They never quite knew when they should get up and when they should go to bed.

One creature did know about light—he had seen it for himself as he flew around the earth. This was the crow, a friendly bird whom everybody liked and trusted.

"I've seen daylight," he said. "It's marvelous. You can see exactly what you're doing, and you don't keep tripping over things. And of course, it's wonderful when you go hunting, because you can see the animals a long way off."

The people's eyes grew round. Daylight was exactly what they needed. It would help them to see the great polar bears who came lumbering up out of the darkness to attack them.

"Go and fetch us some daylight," they said to the crow. "It would solve all our problems. We're tired of living in the dark."

At first the crow was doubtful. "I'm not sure," he said. "The land of daylight is many miles away and would they give me any if I asked?" But the Inuit begged and pleaded, so in the end the crow promised that he would do his best, and away he flew, up into the eastern sky.

After a very long flight the crow noticed that it was getting lighter. He felt hopeful and flew a little faster, dropping down toward a village. Here the people still lived in igloos but the land was light. One of these igloos was bigger than the rest. It belonged to the chief and it was glowing with light. The crow slipped into the branches of a tree to see what was going on.

A woman came out with a bucket. He watched her walk over to the frozen river where she dipped it into a hole in the ice. As she walked back toward the chief's igloo, the crow turned himself into a little speck of dust and floated silently out of the tree. That was how he got inside. You don't often see a crow in a house, but there is always dust!

It was lovely inside the igloo. The chief sat watching his baby grandson play with his toys. These were very beautiful, all made of ivory: little boats called kayaks, carved polar bears and carved whales, and tiny Inuit people and tiny igloos to put them in.

The baby laughed as he played at his grandfather's feet but then, quite suddenly, he screwed up his face and started to wail. A strange voice was whispering in his ear, and something was tickling him. "Tell them to give you some daylight," the voice was saying.

"Daylight," said the baby.

The chief brought down a carved wooden box full of his most precious things. Out of it he took a silver ball, much like the ornaments hung on Christmas trees, but this was shinier than any of those. The baby grabbed it and started to chortle with happiness.

"Now ask for some string," whispered the strange voice.

"String!" said the baby obediently. And his grandfather tied a piece onto the ball for him so he could play. The chief could refuse the child nothing. He was going to be very spoiled when he got a little older.

After a while the baby stood up and toddled out of the igloo into the wintry outside, pulling the silver ball behind him, watching as its wonderful shininess scattered the darkness with flashes of light.

The crow was ready. The speck of dust in the baby's ear

floated away and turned back into a handsome black bird, which took the string in its beak and flew up into the sky.

The baby screamed as his marvelous new toy rose up into the darkness, the long string stretching out and the silver ball bobbling after it. The chief and his hunters shot

arrows at the crow as he flew higher and higher, but he was much too quick for them. On and on he went, breaking little pieces off the silver ball and dropping them onto the lonely dark villages below so that each would have some light. When he reached his own village, he dropped the

ball itself and it broke into hundreds of pieces. Every single house had light now.

"I could only bring one ball of daylight," puffed the crow. "All the daylight there is would have been too heavy for me to carry, I never would have reached home. So you will have to put up with darkness for part of the year. I hope that's all right."

"It's wonderful!" everyone shouted and they ran around in the light, amazed at how easy it was to see things. The Inuit were great hunters but they never tried to harm the crow. He had done them a great service.

-+->-●-<-+-

HOW A BROOMSTICK BRIGHTENED THE WORLD

—◆—

A STORY FROM SRI LANKA

THE SKY WAS NOT ALWAYS as high above the earth as it is today. Indeed, as the sun and the moon traveled around their courses, they often seemed to brush the rooftops, and the stars were so low they were used as lamps outside people's houses.

Once, a servant girl, busy sweeping dust from outside her mistress's house, became very irritated by the passing clouds. They were full of rain and she kept getting her hair wet. They were also much too low and they made everything so dim that she could hardly see.

In the end, she lost her temper. "Go away!" she shouted up at the sky. "I can't do anything with you around. You're making my life impossible," and she whacked the sky with her broomstick.

The sky was a creature of great dignity. He did not like

being shouted at by a cheeky little servant girl. He gathered his cloudy robes around him and withdrew, floating far, far away until he was well out of reach of the broom. And there he has always remained.

He has no intention of getting thrashed again.

In the East it is a great insult to hit somebody with a broom. Even wicked demons are scared of them, so it is handy to have one around. No wonder the sky went well out of danger!

-+->-•-<-+-

Creatures Great and Small

Why Rabbit Is Shy

From the Hopi Tribe of North America

Rabbit was not always shy. Once he was brave and fearless. Once, too, the sun was very different from the way he is now. He was much fiercer, if you can believe that! Here is the story of how they changed their ways, those two creatures, Sun and Rabbit.

It happened long ago in the height of summer. No rain had fallen for many weeks. The rivers had dried up and the trees had withered. All day a huge sun shone down from a hard blue sky. The animals longed for clouds and for rain to fall from them. They had no strength left to hunt for food. All day they crouched in the shadows of the brown trees and the baked, hard rocks, waiting for the end of things. It had never been so hot before.

Rabbit was as unhappy as the rest of them, but he was angry, too. He shook his fist at Sun and shouted, "Go away, this minute! Stop shining for a while. Have pity on us. The earth is drying up. Can't you see what you are doing?"

But Sun took no notice at all. He simply went on pouring his red-hot beams down on the earth.

Rabbit stormed off and sat sulking behind a rock. Then he had a long think. "I know," he said at last, "I'll pick a fight with Sun, and if he doesn't stop shining, I'll kill him."

So he set off for the end of the world, to the place where Sun rose each morning. He was bound to catch him there. He looked very fine in his hunting clothes, in his cloak of white buckskin and the skin of a coyote slung across his shoulders. On his back was a quiver of arrows, sharp enough to kill Sun, and he practiced as he walked along, raising his bow to hit the cactuses and the yucca trees, throwing sticks at the ants and the beetles. By the time he reached the end of the world his aim was very good indeed.

But Sun was not there.

"Coward!" sneered Rabbit. "He's hiding. They must have told him I was on my way." So he hid in some bushes and waited for Sun to come back. But Rabbit soon discovered that catching Sun was no easy matter.

In those days he came up in a rush—one minute it was dark and the next he took a great leap upward, lighting the world in an instant. Rabbit knew that he would have to watch very carefully in order to catch him. So he fit an arrow to his bow and settled down to wait.

Sun decided to play tricks. Rabbit looked so silly in his buckskin cloak and his coyote skin flapping around his shoulders. So Sun did not rise in his usual spot; instead, he kept popping up all over the place, to the right, to the left, now in front, now behind. And however fast Rabbit drew his bow he always aimed too late. Sun had already escaped and was rushing away into the sky. "You'll never catch *me*!" he boasted.

Down below, Rabbit stamped around in fury. It was getting so hot that the animals were dying. He, too, was growing weak, but he knew that he must be patient. Sun would get tired of playing tricks in the end.

Sure enough, after a while, Sun grew lazy and this gave Rabbit his big chance. Stealthily he crept out of hiding, drew his bow, and released an arrow. It flashed through the air, hit Sun, and went in deep.

Rabbit went wild with joy; he rolled about on the ground and gave great whoops of delight. He had done it! He had killed the sun! But after a minute he stopped whooping because he had seen something terrible out of the corner of his eye. Sun was bleeding where Rabbit's arrow had pierced him. Flames were pouring out of a gaping wound in his side and everything seemed to be on fire. In trying to save the world, poor Rabbit had made things worse. He really *was* going to die now.

Away he ran, and the fire swept after him.

"Help me, oh, help me!" he cried to the plants and bushes that lay in his path. "Give me shelter, hide me from these terrible flames."

But they all shook their heads. "We will be burned to ashes if we help you," they said.

Only the little desert brush was brave enough to give him shelter, and that is why, today, it always turns yellow when the sun comes out.

Rabbit, too, changed color. He got little brown spots on his neck where Sun scorched him, and he stopped acting fierce and became timid and shy. His fight with the sun had been much too much for him.

Sun changed, too. He is now so harsh and bright nobody can look at him long enough to aim an arrow. But he is more wary than he used to be. He takes his time, these days, rising in the morning and setting at night. You never know. Rabbit might be waiting for him.

-+->-•-<-+-

WHY SNAKE HAS NO LEGS

An Ashanti Story from Ghana

When the world was still very new, all the animals had legs, except for Snail and he didn't mind because he had a snug little house on his back. All the others had to build their own shelters and they had to feed themselves, too, and grow things.

One day, they decided to build a new farm and plant extra crops. It meant clearing a great big space in the forest and this was hard work, so they agreed to do it together and share the harvest. But on the first day, Snake, who was an idle creature, said that his great aunt was coming to see him and he would have to stay in his hut. The other animals went off to begin cutting down the trees and by nightfall they'd made a good start.

It was no thanks to Snake, though; he really was lazy. The next morning he said he couldn't help because his old mother was sick and needed a visit. On the next day, he said he had a bad cold. Every morning brought a new excuse. The animals grew tired of him, especially when he clambered up a tree and sat watching them all work, being critical and telling them they were doing everything wrong. "Come down and help us, then!" they shouted. But he just walked away to another quiet spot.

All the animals worked hard and at last the crops were planted. After a time, the rains came and everything sprouted, including a lot of weeds. But the animals were

good farmers; they dug and weeded and hoed, and at last a wonderful harvest was ready to gather in. All their hard work had been worthwhile.

But the night before they were to reap the first harvest, a terrible thing happened. Someone came into their plantation and stole the ripened crops. And this happened again and again, night after night. The poor animals were heartbroken and they sent for the spider Kwaku Ananse, because of all creatures, he was by far the cleverest. He listened very carefully and had a long think.

Then he said, "Don't worry, I have a plan. Just be patient and in a week's time you'll have caught this thief, I promise."

Ananse went home and asked his son, Ntikuma, to help him. Together they collected some barrels of tar and when it was night, they rolled them to the animals' new farm and spread the tar in great patches all around the ripest crops. Then son Ntikuma was sent home to bed. Father Ananse climbed into a tree and kept watch.

It grew very still and silent, and the spider nearly fell asleep, but then, just as he was nodding off, a loud noise woke him, a sound of grunting and heaving, a sound of someone cursing. It was Snake and he was stuck in the middle of a patch of tar!

Ananse slipped silently down from his tree and went home to his village, leaving the thief to struggle with the horrible stickiness. He knew Snake would never get free without some help. Serves him right, thought the clever spider.

Next day he summoned all the animals and they set off for their farm to see what had happened to Snake.

He was still stuck firmly in the tar but the other animals showed him no mercy. They grabbed long sticks and beat him till he squealed.

"Thief!" they shouted. "Fat lazy thief!" Then, stepping carefully between the tar patches, they went off to harvest the crops that were left.

The next morning they came back with some pieces of rope. Ananse the spider led the way. They made a dirt path across the tar and tied the ropes around Snake. In those days he was short and fat. (No wonder, since he just sat and watched other people work.) When everything was in place, the animals pushed flat sticks underneath his body to try and unstick him. "Pull!" Ananse shouted and they all tugged on the ropes. Nothing at all happened and Snake began to whimper with fear. "Harder!" cried Ananse. "Pull harder!" So the animals pulled and pulled and PULLED.

For a long time Snake did not come out of the tar patch; he just grew longer and longer. Then there was a most peculiar sucking noise and, *gloopity-gloop*, he was free at last. As he came whooshing out of the tar all the animals fell backward on top of one another, in a heap.

There was silence for a minute or two, then everybody stared at Snake. He looked so very odd. What was wrong with him? What was different?

"He has no legs!" cried Ananse, and do you know, he had left them behind in the tar. That wasn't all—the stretching had made him terribly long and thin.

They carried him to his house and took care of him until everything had healed. Poor Snake sat and waited for his legs to grow again. But they never did. And that's why, to this day, he has to go everywhere on his stomach, hiding in dark secret places because he is ashamed of himself.

→>•<←

WHY THE BEAR HAS A STUMPY TAIL

A STORY FROM NORWAY

ONE DAY BEAR MET FOX. Fox was slinking along as usual, his mouth stuffed with fish.

"Where did you get those fish?" said Bear. It was winter and food was hard to find. He was extremely hungry. He had never tried catching a fish but he was determined to learn. A few fat fish would make him a tasty meal.

"It's very easy," Fox told him. But he didn't like Bear very much and he decided to play a trick on him. "All you do is find a lake and slide across the ice till you reach the middle. You cut a hole and you sit down, and you stick your tail into the water. It stings a little but you must leave it there as long as you can because when it stings, the fish will start biting. They're curious creatures, so they'll soon come up to see what's happening. The longer you can stay there the more fish you'll catch. They'll hang on to your tail.

When you've caught some you just give it a little twist and out they come. Got it?"

"Got it," said Bear and he shambled off to find a lake. It sounded very easy. His mouth was watering as he banged at the ice with his huge furry paws and he'd soon made a nice big hole. Sitting on the edge, he stuck in his lovely long tail and waited.

Just how long he sat there Bear could never say. He got so cold that his rear end went numb. As for his tail, he couldn't feel it at all and there was no way of telling if he'd caught any fish. He grew tired in the end, and stood up in a huff.

Snap! Bear peered down at the frozen lake. No fish. No tail either. It had frozen solid and broken right off. All he had left was a funny little stump.

-+->-•-<-+-

WHY ELEPHANTS LIVE IN THE JUNGLE

FROM THE KAMBA PEOPLE OF KENYA

THERE WAS ONCE A MAN who was desperately poor. His clothes were ragged and he had big holes in his sandals. He was always hungry, too, because there was never any money to buy food. One day he went to see his witch doctor.

"I need some magic," he said, "some magic so I can make some money. I'm tired of being poor."

"Go and see Ivonya-ngia," advised the witch doctor. "He will help you, he's very rich indeed."

So the man tramped off to the village where Ivonya-ngia lived and found him surrounded by all his cattle. When he saw the poor man in his rags, the rich man's heart melted.

"Give him goats," he ordered his men. "Give him sheep and cows. I have plenty to spare. That should give him a good start in life."

But the man shook his head. "I don't want your charity,"

he said ungratefully, "I want to become rich on my own. What's the secret?"

"Hard work," said the rich farmer.

"I just want magic," the poor man grumbled. He was in a hurry.

The farmer became thoughtful. Then he dug among his robes and took out a little jar of ointment.

"Go home to your wife," he said. "Rub this on her eye-teeth, those two pointy ones in the top of her jaw. It will make them grow and when they're long enough you can sell them. They'll be pure ivory and that is worth a lot of money."

The poor man was greedy and rushed home at once, grabbed his wife, and rubbed the magic ointment all over her pointy teeth. Then he waited. Sure enough the teeth began to grow. He sat there all day and all night just watching her, his excitement mounting, with pictures of money bags floating through his head. And the teeth grew longer and longer.

At last they slowed down, then stopped altogether. When the man was sure the magic had finished its work, he got some pincers and pulled out the teeth. Then he carried them to the market and sold them for a lot of money. He had become rich overnight.

The man next door was jealous. He was poor, too, and as greedy as his neighbor. He went to see the same farmer straight away, came home with the same magic ointment, and rubbed it all over his wife's teeth. But he'd been in such a hurry to get rich that he hadn't bothered to listen carefully enough to the farmer's instructions. He hadn't heard that he had to pull the teeth *out* and the silly man just let them go on growing and growing.

You can imagine what happened next. As the poor woman's teeth grew steadily longer, she herself began to change. Her skin became thick and coarse, her ears turned into two huge flaps and her nose became so long she could pick things up from the floor with it. She was soon so enormous that the walls of their little mud hut burst open and fell flat and, before long, she charged off into the jungle. You know why, don't you? Yes, she had turned into an elephant!

Soon after this she had a baby son and he was an elephant, too. She was much happier in the jungle without that greedy husband of hers back home. Elephants are wiser than people, and she never went back to him.

→>●<←

WHY THERE ARE BUTTERFLIES

AN AUSTRALIAN ABORIGINAL STORY

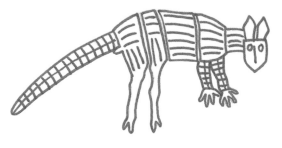

THIS HAPPENED WHEN THERE were only animals on earth. No people. And the animals were very happy because they did not know about death. But one day something terrible happened. A young cockatoo who was just learning to fly fell out of a tree and broke his neck. He lay on the ground like a jewel, all glowing against the green forest floor, not breathing, the warmth gradually fading from his feathers.

None of the animals could understand it. What was happening to the little cockatoo? Where had he gone? They all tried to wake him up, opening his eyes and prodding him very gently. But there was no life in him at all.

They sent for the owl, the wisest of all the birds, but he could not help them.

Neither could the eagle. All he did was to throw a pebble into the river. As it disappeared into the water he cried, "See, it has passed from one existence into another. So has the little cockatoo."

So they sent for the crow. He took a stick and dropped that into the river. It vanished for a second but then bobbed up again. "There," said the crow, "we do not need to worry about death. We go into another existence like Eagle said, but we come back again."

The animals were comforted by this. At least death did not mean you disappeared forever. But they wanted to know more. "We must put this to the test," they said. "Who will copy poor Cockatoo? Who will close his eyes and lie very still, not speaking or hearing or seeing or eating, for a long, long time, then come back to us, perhaps in some other shape?"

"I will," cried the snake.

"So will I," cried the wombat, the opossum, and the goanna. And when winter came they all crept away, curled up in a dark warm place, and went to sleep.

When spring returned, all the animals gathered together and waited to see what had happened. The sleeping creatures came wandering along, very thin and dazed looking. All seemed much the same except that the snake was wearing a different skin. Everyone was disappointed. This had not really solved the great mystery of death.

"Let us try," said the insects, the grubs and the water-bugs, the caterpillars and the beetles, but they were laughed at. They were so small and feeble, they had no brains at all.

"Well, you *can*," Eagle said doubtfully (he was in charge), "but I don't suppose you will get very far."

"Thank you, sir," said the insects politely and they crept away. The waterbugs wrapped themselves in bark and floated off down the river. Others crept into the trunks of trees or slipped into the ground. But before they disappeared they made a promise: "We will come back next spring in a different form," they told the larger animals. "Meet us in the mountains."

Winter came and everyone became sleepy and slow, but when the earth began to warm up again, there was an excitement in the air.

One by one the animals began to travel toward the mountains. They met in a great clearing among the trees, which had already sprouted fresh green leaves in their honor. The dragonflies went all over the place, reminding everybody that it was time to greet the bugs and the caterpillars, who had promised to return in a new shape. Better still, they had promised to take away the awful terror of death.

As the sun rose, the animals who had gathered together in the clearing fell silent. The dragonflies were coming back but this time they were not alone. They flew at the head of what seemed at first like a great cloud of gorgeous color—many, many colors, every color on earth. As the cloud drew near it began to separate into smaller clouds and these clouds grew ever smaller, until they were mere puffs, like leaves, like specks of light.

Each one glowed with its own special brightness, and rested on trees and bushes and plants. The marvels were butterflies.

At first the watching animals could hardly speak; then they began to cry aloud, praising the creator of the butterflies, who had shown them that death was not dark and cold but that it meant new life.

And for the first time since the world began,
all the birds started singing.

BIBLIOGRAPHY

Appiah, Peggy. *Tales of an Ashanti Father*. Illustrated by Mona Dickson. Boston: Beacon Press, 1989.

Asbjornson, Peter Christen. *Popular Tales from the Norse*. Translated by Sir George Webbe Dasent. New York: Putnam, 1912.

Bierhorst, John, ed. *Myths and Tales of the American Indians*. New York: Farrar, Straus & Giroux, 1976. Reprint, New York: Indian Head Books, 1992.

Crossley-Holland, Kevin. *The Norse Myths*. New York: Pantheon Books, 1980.

Freund, Philip. *Myths of Creation*. Illustrated by Milton Charles. New York: Washington Square Press, 1965.

Grimal, Pierre, ed. *Larousse World Mythology*. Translated by Patricia Beardsworth. New York: Putnam, 1965.

Hamilton, Virginia. *In the Beginning: Creation Stories from Around the World*. Illustrated by Barry Moser. New York: Harcourt Brace, 1988.

Hayes, Barbara. *Folk Tales and Fables of Asia and Australia*. Illustrated by Robert Ingpen. New York: Chelsea House Publishers, c. 1994.

Hayes, Barbara. *Folk Tales and Fables of the Americas and the Pacific*. Illustrated by Robert Ingpen. New York: Chelsea House Publishers, c. 1994.

Hull, Robert. *Norse Stories: Tales from Around the World*. Illustrated by Jonathon Heap and Adam Stower. New York: Thomson Learning, 1993.

Knappert, Jan. *Kings, Gods, and Spirits from African Mythology*. Illustrated by Francesca Pelizzoli. New York: Schocken Books, 1986. Reprint, New York: Peter Bedrick Books, 1993.

Parker, Henry. *Village Folk-Tales of Ceylon*. Vol. 1. Edited by Richard M. Dorson. 1910. Reprint, Salem, N.H.: Ayer, 1977.

Pilling, Ann. *Before I Go to Sleep: A Collection of Bible Stories, Poems, and Prayers for Children*. Illustrated by Katy M. Denton. New York: Crown Books, 1990.

Sanders, Tao Tao Liu. *Dragons, Gods, and Spirits from Chinese Mythology*. New York: Schocken Books, 1983. Reprint, New York: Peter Bedrick Books, 1994.

Smith, W. Ramsay. *Myths and Legends of the Australian Aboriginals*. 1930. Reprint, New York: Johnson Reprint Corp., 1970.

Spence, Lewis. *The Myths of North American Indians*. New York: Farrar and Rinehart, 1932.

Wood, Marion. *Spirits, Heroes, and Hunters from North American Indian Mythology*. Illustrated by John Sibbick. New York: Schocken Books, 1982, c. 1981. Reprint, New York: Peter Bedrick Books, 1992.

Introduction quotation from Robert Frost, preface to *Collected Poems* (1939).

Permission granted to reproduce "How the World Was Made in Seven Days," originally titled "God Makes the World," from *Before I Go to Sleep* by Ann Pilling, published by Kingfisher. Published in the U.S. by Crown Books. Copyright © 1990 by Ann Pilling.